IN THE NEXT ROOM

MATSUKI MASUTANI

増谷松樹

I WILL BE MORE MYSELF IN THE NEXT WORLD

POEMS

Mother Tongue Publishing Limited
Salt Spring Island, BC
Canada

MOTHER TONGUE PUBLISHING LIMITED
290 Fulford-Ganges Road, Salt Spring Island, B.C. V8K 2K6 Canada
www.mothertonguepublishing.com
Represented in North America by Heritage Group Distribution.

Book Design by Mark Hand.
Cover, a reduction linocut "From Tumbo Island" by Mimi Fujino.
Author photograph by Brian Grogan.
Printed on Natural Cream, Rolland Enviro, FSC certified.
Printed and bound in Canada.

Mother Tongue Publishing acknowledges the assistance of the Province of
British Columbia through the B.C. Arts Council. We acknowledge the support
of the Canada Council for the Arts. Thank-you. Nous remercions le Conseil des
arts du Canada de son soutien.

LIBRARY AND ARCHIVES CANADA CATALOGUING IN PUBLICATION

Title: I will be more myself in the next world : poems / Matsuki Masutani.
Names: Masutani, Matsuki, author.
Description: Poems in English; includes Japanese translations of selected
poems.
Identifiers: Canadiana 20210162856 | ISBN 9781896949871 (softcover)
Classification: LCC PS8626.A8225 I2 2021 | DDC C811/.6–dc23

For my wife, Jane;
my children, Hanako, Masaki, Akiko;
my grandchildren, Eiko, Ren, Naoki, Soren, Mei;
and my parents in the other world
my life and inspiration

妻ジェーン
子供たち、花子、正樹、アキコ
孫の瑛子、蓮、直樹、ソーレン、メイ
そして他界した父母
に捧ぐ

I am

more than
my body
more than
what I think.
I am
more than
what I do
what I did
and what I will do.

Actually
I am
more than
what I am
in this world
and I feel
I will be
more myself
in the next
world.

CONTENTS

MARRIAGE

結婚生活

i.

I met my wife

in Kathmandu
and we wandered together
many months
reaching Canada
where we stopped
but stayed in the travellers' lifestyle.
Even after raising three kids
we are in traveller's mode
bumbling around
in cafés and thrift shops
in the neighbourhood
going nowhere.

i.

旅の途中

ネパールで
妻に出会った。
いっしょに
長い旅をして
カナダに着いた。
そこで旅は終わったが
旅人のような暮らしは続いた。
三人の子供をそだてた後も
生活は変らず
近所のカフェーや
古着屋をほっつき歩くだけで
どこにも行かなかった。

ii.

My wife says

"You are
in front of your desk
all the time
from morning till night
day after day
year after year
it's obviously an old habit.
I think we should
do something
more dynamic
than that before
it's too late."

ii.

「いつも

いつも
机の前に
朝から
夜まで
くる日も
くる日も
くる年も
くる年も
座っている。
明らかに
古くからの習性だから
手遅れにならないうちに
何か
ダイナミックなことを
するべきヨ」
と妻は言う。

iii.

Emphasize the positive

neglect the negative.
Such a simple
way to survive
is incomprehensible
to my wife,
who insists
on facing life
head on
with all her emotions.
She complains,
"Life is hard for me.
People all around
are turning into robots."

I'm jealous of her
rich emotional life.

iii.

ポジティブを

強調し
ネガティブを
無視する
こんな簡単な
処世術が
妻には
わからないらしい
そして
人生には
本当の感情を以って
正面から
向い合うべきだと主張する。
そして
「あたしの人生は苦しい。周りの人が、どんどんロボットになっ
てゆく」
と嘆く。

妻の豊かな感情生活が羨ましいときもある。

iv.

Loudly

she came careering up
the driveway
lurched the truck to a stop
leapt out in pink
pants and a purple shirt
black handbag in her right hand
left arm slicing the air
she blasted through the gate
and walked into the house
shouting, "I'm back!"

iv.

騒音を立てて

ドライブウェイを
まっすぐに
走って来て
右に大きく切る。
トラックを止めると
ドアを開けて
跳び出してくる。
ピンクのパンツに
パープルのシャツ
右手に
黒のハンドバックを持ち
左手で空を切りながら
風のように
ゲートを抜けて
「タダイマ」
と大声を挙げて
家に
入ってくる。

v.

Suddenly

as if
responding to
my prayer,
a phone call
came
telling me about a
translation job.
A few emails flew around
and I was
a different person.
I became a
highly stressed
self-centered husband,
telling my wife
what to do.

V.

突然

まるで
祈りに
応えるかのように
電話が入り
イメールを交換する。
そうして仕事が入ってくると
僕は
別人のようになる。
ストレス過多の
自己中心的な
ハズバンドに変り、
あれこれ
妻に
注文をつける。

vi.

I was at my computer

My wife was downstairs
at her computer.
She shouted,
"I don't know
what to do!"
I shouted back,
"Dust the kitchen
light fixture,"
remembering she always says,
"I should dust that light."
I expected she would say,
"No way!"
But she said, "Okay,"
and put on CBC radio.
Relieved,
I went to have a nap.

vi.

僕が

コンピュータに向かっていると
階下から
妻が叫ぶ。
「何もすることないわ!」
僕は叫び返した。
「キッチンのランプをそうじしたら」
(あの埃を何とかしなきゃ)
と妻が言っていたのを思い出したからだ。
「冗談じゃない」と言うだろうと思っていたが、
妻が「オーケー」と言って
ラジオをつけた。
僕は安心して
昼寝をした。

vii.

In her dream

my wife said
I abandoned her
in the middle
of a strange city
forcing her
out of our car.
She had
a hell of a time
trying to get home.
I should apologize
somehow.

vii.

夢の中で

僕が
妻を
自動車から
追い出して
見知らぬ街に
置いてきぼりにしたという
家に帰りつくのが
とても大変だった
と言う。
どう謝ったらいいのだろうか？

viii.

I woke up

from a nap
remembering the sensation
of driving fast
around a sharp
curve.
But I could not
remember where
I was going.
It was as if
the road had vanished
right in front
of my speeding car.
It bothered me
and I recalled
my wife saying
that people who take
naps tend to lose
their minds.

viii.

昼寝から

醒めると
急カーブを
急速度で
運転していた
感覚が残っているが
どこに向かっていたのかは
ぜんぜん記憶になかった。
まるで
疾走する
車の真ん前から
道路が消滅したかのようで
気味悪かった。
昼寝をする人には惚ける人が多い、
と妻がいっていたのを
思い出した。

ix.

As my wife chatters on

I keep my silence
playing out
my role
of silent partner,
allowing her
to speak
for us.
This habit
goes back
to the beginning.
I couldn't speak
English without
her aid.

But now,
I am bored
with my role
and seek
an opportunity
to interject.

ix.

妻がお喋りを続ける横で

僕は沈黙を守り
無口のパートナーという
自分の役割を演じる。
こうやって
僕らの話は
妻がはなすという
この習慣は
僕が
妻の助けがないと
英語がしゃべれなかった
最初の頃まで
さかのぼる。
しかしこの頃は
この役割にも飽きてきて
口をはさむ
機会を探している。

x.

On the way back

from a party,
I was suffering
excruciating stomach pains.
My wife,
drunk,
was telling me
how much
she loves me
how much
she feels bad
for me.
I thought
I was dying.

Then she said,
"Capricorn men always have stomach problems.
Do you know why?"
I replied,
"We don't say what we want to say."
"What do you want to say now?"
"Shut up!"
But she kept talking
and giggling.
I still thought
I was dying.

x.

パーティーからの

帰り路
僕は腹痛で
苦しんでいた。
酔っぱらっている
妻は
どんなに愛しているかとか
どんなに同情しているかとか
繰り返し言うが
僕は堪らなく
苦しかった。

しばらくして
「山羊座の男は胃腸に問題があるっていうけど、
どうしてなのかしら?」
と妻が言うので
「言いたいことを言わないからだよ」
と答えた。
「今は何を言いたいの?」
「うるさい!」
しかし
妻はおしゃべりも
くすくす笑いも
止めなかった。
僕は死ぬのほど
苦しかった。

xi.

Today

my Canadian wife,
irritated with me again,
said, "I feel like
I am with an idiot."

After twenty-five years
I still look right then left
whenever I cross a road,
an old habit formed
by crossing too many Japanese roads
for too many years,
partly.

In grade one my favourite
teacher asked us to raise
our right hands.
I raised my left.
When she said "left,"
I raised my right
while everyone else
swiftly and confidently
raised their hands correctly.
She thought I was joking,
but in fact I was frozen with fear.

My wife knows the story,
but it still bothers her,
and she says,
"Next time
I'll marry somebody
more normal."

xi.

今日も

カナダ人の妻は
僕に苛立って言った。
「まるで阿呆といっしょにいるみたい」
もうカナダに来て数十年経つが
道を横切る時
まず右を見てから左を見る。
これは何十年も
日本の道を渡った癖だ。

小学一年生の時
大好きだった先生が
クラスのみんなに
右手を上げるように言った時
僕だけ左手を上げた。
先生が左手というと
右手を上げた。
クラスのみんなは素早く元気に
いわれたように手をあげていた。
先生は僕がふざけていると思ったらしいが
僕は緊張して凍りついていた。

妻もこの話は知っているが、
それでも我慢できないらしい。
「この次は、もっと普通の人と結婚するわ」
と言う。

xii.

I say "We"

meaning my wife and I.
She also says
"We" meaning
her and me.
Sometimes
they are significantly different.
"We" could be happy
and unhappy
at the same time.
I shouldn't worry about it too much
until she stops saying "We."

xii.

僕が

「僕たち」というと
僕と妻とのこと。
妻が「ワタシたち」というと
妻と僕とのこと
この二つが
極端に違うこともある。
一方がハッピーなのに
もう一方がハッピーでないこともある。
どっちにしても
妻が「ワタシたち」と言っている間は
心配ない。

xiii.

A young woman asked me,

"What is the secret of a long marriage?"
I replied,
"If both fall out of love at the same time,
that will be the end of it.
But if one of you is still in love,
It might go on."
She said,
"That sucks!"
So I added,
"marriages change."
and I thought of all the struggles
we'd gone through.
It's not like
they had ended.
A week later
I saw the young woman
with a new dog
and she looked
happy.

xiii.

長い結婚の秘訣は何?

と若い女性が尋ねた
それで僕は答えた。
「同時に二人とも嫌になったら
それで終わりになるけど、
一人にでも未練があるなら
それは続く」
そんなの嫌!
と、言うから
「でも状況はどんどん変わるよ」
と言った。
そして僕と妻とが辿った
数々の葛藤を想った。
それが終わったわけではないが、、、。
一週間後、
彼女が新しい犬を連れているのを見た。
前よりも
うれしそうだった。

JAPAN

I'm living an unexpected

life an ocean away
from my lot in Japan.
Sometimes I imagine
there's still an empty seat
at the table
waiting for me
after forty years.

Like my brothers

I went abroad
but I did not return.
My mother thought
I was fooling around and just
forgot to come home.
My parents wanted me
to be a scholar,
like my father
but secretly,
I wanted to be
a bohemian.

When hippies appeared
I escaped from Japan
to Nepal.
I met a girl
with a nose ring
and moved to Canada.

I ran away

from my father
to find out
who I was.
Now, forty
years later,
I look back
at my father
and wonder
who he was.

I'm a half-man

speaking half-English,
lacking the skills
of a real man
to make a living
or fix things
or to be
generally capable.

My older brothers
hung around father
and developed
manly skills
and temperaments.
I was too small,
and a nuisance.
I hung out
with my mum and sister
and learned
to cook
and chat
and be happy just
hanging out.

I looked up
to my father
from a distance
and considered myself
the heir to
his monkish pursuits.
I worshipped my father
as though he was descended from
the most noble clan
in the country.

He was a poor
writer and when
he met my mother
he already had a wife
and three children.
After marrying her
he became respectable,

and a leading scholar.
Together they had
four children.
Forty years later
I am a poor
poet. I have stayed
with my wife
and three children
and I have struggled.

During a separation
from my wife,
the image of my
young mother appeared
and gazed at me
silently, as if to say
"This is your call."

Meanwhile
my real mother,
old and alive
across the Pacific Ocean,
had no idea of the struggles
in my life.
And at the time I knew nothing of
my father's first marriage.

Lately

I see my father
in the mirror.
It is weird to see
his stern expression
on my face.
I don't know
how to take it.
Behind this face,
behind the semblance of the ordinary,
he blindsided us.
We did not see his other life,
a family of three children
until his demise.

On his deathbed,
he was confused
and asked me,
"Tell me, who is your mother?"
I pointed and said,
"She's in the kitchen, downstairs."
He couldn't hear me well, and panicked,
"Excuse me, but what is your mother's name?
Who? What
is her name?" He was almost stuttering.
He sank into his bed
drowning in a sea of confusion.
I threw him a life raft.
"I'm from Canada," I said.
He became calm.
"Oh yes," he said. "You went
to graduate studies,
but stumbled and left
for an island.
Glad to see you!"
I smiled, relieved
by his safe landing.

My half-sister said

our father counted on me
to try hard to the end
without ever giving up.

I was surprised to hear this.
I thought he'd lost hope for me
long ago, after seeing
my failures
one after another.

Apparently, he had
not been disappointed.
He told her,
"He is doing his own thing,"
as if he was pleased
and amused. He told her,
"He is like me."

I came to a foreign land

married
a foreigner.
I live with foreigners.
It's a strange thing to do.
My mother said
in her last letter
"I lost track
of your life."
I read this
and wondered,
Where am I?
Who was
my mother?

My mother's life

escapes me.
I remember
her face, soft smile
and common sense.
Only after her death
did I realize
she had another
face, hidden,
more passionate
and determined.
I must have been
self-absorbed
and foolish
not to have noticed
this earlier.

1970 Kawasaki, Japan

you passed away
at sunrise
with an apology to your parents,
echoing Vietnamese monks,
you prayed, meditated
and set yourself on fire to protest the raging
imperial war.
You were twenty-one.

Your father was a steel co.
executive, probably profiting
from the war.
In his grief he invited us,
your friends,
all student radicals,
to a fine Japanese restaurant
to commemorate you,
his only son.
He said, "Please
drink and talk
as if my son were
with us."

After the feast
we made a circle for the last time.
The radical movement
was in chaotic decline.
I remember
one of us broke
the silence,
"Let's not forget
he is part of us."

Unexpectedly
we had to carve out
new lives for ourselves
for better or worse.
Most of us quit
university.
Some even
left the country.

In India I thought

I was on my way
to achieving something
earth-shattering.
My ambition was
to equal or exceed
my father's accomplishments.

I met a young woman
who dreamt of a happy
ordinary life in Canada.
She would be a nurse
and I would be
a lab technician.
I thought about a life
of trying not to shatter
test tubes
and decided her dream
was better than mine.

We married and moved
to a small island, and I became
a freelance translator
instead of a lab technician.
We lived a frugal life.

I thought I'd walked away
from my own ambition
forever, but it kept
haunting me
through the years,
rocking our otherwise
ordinary life until
I realized one day
it is indeed earth-shattering
to keep this ordinary life
from shattering.

ISLAND LIFE

島の生活

Long ago in a classroom

I heard about
a utopia called
"the Village of Peach Blossoms."

Many of my friends,
even the girls,
soon dismissed this as fantasy.
But I never forgot
the image.

Now
I realize
I am in it.
I am inside that image,
standing in a garden of apple blossoms.

To get here
I left my country,
my city life,
even my career.

I must be nuts.

At midnight

my wife looked out
the bathroom window.
Our fence was on fire.
I'd started it
with woodstove ashes
I'd carelessly dumped
on the compost.

If she hadn't gone
to the bathroom,
if she hadn't believed
what she saw—the flames
looked like a trick of the light—
and if our well hadn't had enough water...
It shatters me to think
how many times I have escaped
serious consequences
by chance.

After our firefighting,
we saw for the first time
the green of the northern lights
shimmering across the sky,
like a curtain
opening.

I wake up early

and make a fire, clouds
of white rising
from the neighbouring
marsh. I cook fried
rice for the kids
a morning scene
repeated. They are dreaming
and striving
to become somebody.
Girl, boy, girl: vet,
scientist, teacher.

I did not become a professor
Like my father. I did not
Become a writer. Lost now
in middle age on foreign soil,
out of work. I did not
become anyone.

What to do
except pray
on my knees
in front of my menorah.
Is this my consolation
or my fate?

I am the great-grandson of a man
who joined a revolutionary war. He
injured his leg and left
the battlefield. He stayed
in an abandoned
village temple, praying
for his comrades
who sacrificed their lives
for their dreams.

He met a woman and
married her. They had
three children: girl,
boy, girl.

My fourteen-year-old daughter

asked me, "Dad, do you worry
about losing our respect?"
"No! Not at all," I replied.
"That's good."
She sounded relieved.

In bed, I wondered what she meant.
Soon a watchman in a dark costume
appeared and gazed
at the lake of my consciousness,
as if to prevent
a dragon from emerging.

The watchman's earnestness
prevented me from sleeping
for a long time.

In spite of

cloudy skies,
my wife and I
have a great time
in the city,
visiting friends
and restaurants,
feeling happy
and free.
My wife helps
a blind old man
cross the street.

We drive home
in the afternoon
feeling like
butterflies
or dragonflies,
light and happy.

The next day
back at home
on the island,
we fight over
our old theme
"To move or not to move."

One afternoon

my wife opened the door
to find our cat
dragging herself
by her front legs,
her back half lifeless
as an empty sack.

I thought I was looking at
a Japanese ghost.
They walk around
without legs over there.

I looked at the cat
with a radical solution in mind,
and she instantly shot me
back a look of horror.

The cat wasn't in pain.
Just as the vet said it would,
life gradually came back
to her hind legs.

A human spine
can't heal
like that.

I went on a protest walk

to keep my friend company,
and helped another friend
carry a sign.

During the walk
a poet from Quadra Island
read me his Zen poem
and gave me
his book,
The Meaning of Life.

A few days later, I saw myself
on the front page of a local paper,
holding the big sign
I hadn't made:
"No Compliance!"

I feel more conscious

of being different
today because I know
everyone knows
what happened yesterday
in our small town.
Three white guys shouted
at a black guy,
"Get out of our white town
or we're gonna lynch you!"
and tried to beat him up.
It was on the CBC
national news.
The black guy said,
"It's happening
every day
to Asians
and Natives
as well."

I asked a friend
why the names
of the three white guys
weren't revealed,
only the name
of the victim?
He paused and replied,
"I don't know."

I tore my hip muscle

went to town limping,
and noticed many other people
also limping. I had not
noticed them before.

As we rocked on rough waves

I said to myself, "What would
my mother think of me
dying on a sailboat?"

I got more scared and clung
to the rails, praying
in silence, leaving control
of the boat to a priest
I barely knew.

Finally, I said, "Is the worst
over?"

Cupping his hand to his ear,
he smiled.

I'd planned for
a different kind
of sailing, packing
my flute
and a book.

At a party

a man asked me gently,
"Did I meet you
on the garden tour?"
I responded firmly
"No, that was Yoshi.
I'm Matsuki."

I am one of two
Japanese men on the island.
I have long hair and Yoshi's is short.
He wears glasses and I don't.
Still, many people
mix us up.
When people ask me,
"Do you make miso?"
(which Yoshi does)
I say,
"Almost."

The ponytailed woman

smiled and said, "I have five horses
and three ponies.
They certainly give me
something to do."
There was a box at the end
of the driveway with eggs for sale
and magnificent roses and dahlias
blooming in front of the house
where she lives with her aged mother.
Next door her brother lives with his wife
and teaches yoga. They wear white
turbans. Secretly, I
call them "the white Sikhs."

I went for a long walk

in Denman's Central Park.
The view is so monotone, I ended
up looking into my own
mind. Ideas emerged
like clouds sometimes,
shedding a new light
on incidents in my life
as if they had secret
meanings.
I felt like I was walking
the maze of my own brain.

As if it were your wedding

people are abandoning
the living for you, coming
from everywhere, the States, England,
Toronto and Vancouver,
to pay their last respects.

We are writing eulogies,
choosing clothes
and hymns. All day
long, all the time
you're in our minds, more
vividly than ever,
as if you'd moved there.

Here you are again

in my dream.
Meanwhile
my real
father and
my father-
in-law
hardly ever
appear.

During lunch
you keep shaking
your head,
as if telling
me something.
After lunch
you disappear
on an old bicycle
swiftly and deftly.

When I wake up
I realize
never in your life
did you ride
a bike.

But it suited
you so well,
as if, over there
you ride a bike
all the time.

Fog

I woke to thick fog
covering the field.
I felt I was still
in my dream so I
went downstairs
washed my face
made a cup of coffee
returned to the window
to discover the fog
had vanished completely.
I'd been tricked.

CHEMO

抗がん剤治療

i.

Two weeks before
the doctor told me
I had cancer,
the seven gods of luck appeared
in my dream. They came
down the river in a pink boat and docked
in a bed of reeds.
Outside the boat
they had a meeting
and seemed to decide
to help me.
So when the doctor said cancer,
I thought, this is tough
love from the gods,
and did not lose hope.

i.

癌だと告げられる
二週間前
夢の中に
古代の神々が
現れた。
桃色の舟で
河を下ってきて
葦の洲に止め
舟から出て
円陣になって
何事かを話していた。
どうやら僕を助ける相談らしかった。
鋭い目をした医者から
直腸癌を告げられた時
これはあの神々から与えられた試練だと
直観した。

ii.

From my chemo chair
I see the mountains
capped with snow.
It occurs to me:
I am seventy-three years old
I have cancer
I am dying.

The doctor says
I will live.
He is young.

They give me a bottle
with chemo in it.
It will hang from my neck
and I must embrace it.

I am afraid
of the bottle with its tubes
but it is the water of life.
The nurse calls it a baby bottle.

I must make my life more worthy.

ii.

抗がん剤治療の
安楽椅子に
ゆったりと座って
雪を被った山々と
その上に浮かぶ
やわらかそうな雲を
眺めていた。
その時、不思議な幸福感に包まれて
ふと思った。
私はもう七十三 歳で
癌を病んでいる。
死んでもおかしくない。
だが若い医師は
治療すれば大丈夫だという。
それを聞いて
新たに生きようと思った。

病院での注入が終わると
抗がん液の入った瓶を渡された。
看護婦はスラングで「ベイビーボトル」と呼ぶらしい
その瓶を首から吊るして
胸に抱き
四十六時間
自分で注入を続ける。
最初は、細い管が付いたこの瓶が恐ろしかったが、
だんだん慣れて
生命の水のようだ
と思うようになった。

iii.

If I have a fever
over 38 degrees, the nurse
says I must go
to Emergency,
immediately.

"But Emergency is crowded,"
I tell her.
She smiles and says,
"Don't worry.
You are a chemo patient.
You can jump the queue."

I stiffen.
I cannot imagine myself
in an ambulance.
I cannot imagine myself
jumping over the queue.

iii.

もしも
八度以上の熱がでたら
すぐに
救急にいくんですよ
と
看護婦がいう。

でも
救急は混雑しているん
でしょうと
顔を顰めると、
看護婦は
その心配はありませんよ。
あなたは、癌ですから、
待たずに済みます
と元気よくいう。

ギョ、ギョ
救急車で運ばれて
救急患者の列を飛び越えるなんて
とんでもない
と
身を硬くした。

iv.

I try to listen
to the movement
of chemo in my body
to calm myself.
It fills my abdomen and heart
Saaaaaaa....
A tidal flow of ocean water
at night, reflecting the moon.

iv.

僕は
心を
しずめて
液の動きに
注意を
傾ける
お腹から
肺の方に
サササササーと
満ちて
その夜の海に
月が
浮かぶ

v.

I'm losing my hair.
Every time I touch my head
white hairs fall to my sweater.
The nurse says,
"In a few months,
it will grow back,
maybe in a different color,
even black."

I look in the mirror
and see an old face.
It is hard to believe
it is me.
It is hard to believe
I have cancer.

In my long gaze,
the person in the mirror
becomes someone else.

V.

頭に
手をやるたびに
パラパラと
白髪が落ちてくる
「数ケ月もすれば
また生えてきますよ。
黒髪が生えてくるかもしれない」
と看護婦は言う。
鏡の中には
髪が薄くなった
自分の顔が見える
自分がこんなに老いるなんて
自分が癌だなんて
信じられない。
そう思って
眺めていると
鏡の中の顔が
他人のように見えてくる。

vi.

A small frame appears
around my world
which makes it more
picturesque
and remote
as if it were al-
ready in the past,
a memory.

At night
a river flows
in the frame.
Sometimes its dark
waters dance.

vi.

ぼくの世界に
小さな
額ぶちが現れて
世界を
縁どる。
縁どられた世界は
絵のように
美しく
記憶のように
懐かしい。
夜になると
その額ぶちの中を
河が流れる。
その暗い水が
咆えることもある。

vii.

From my living room
window I watch
an old cherry tree blossom
day after day.

One afternoon
two young girls
sit under the tree
and drink and eat.
They watch the blossoms
just like in Japan.

When the wind blows
flower petals swarm like insects
and a cyclist flies down the road like a bird.
I am quiet and the tree
stretches out its neck
to ask how I am doing.

vii.

くる日も
くる日も
リビングルームに座って
窓から
桜を眺めていた。
ボッとしていると
桜の方から
首を伸ばして
僕のようすを
覗きにくる。
風が吹くと
花びらが
昆虫のように
舞い
その横を
サイクリストが
鳥のように疾走した。
ある日
ふたりの女の子が
日本でのように
桜の下に座って
飲み食いをした。
カナダ人の孫は
びっくりして
それを眺めていた。

PARKINSON'S

パーキンソン病

i.

In the middle

of my cancer treatment
I saw myself leaving
this world and realized
leaving means losing
everything—
my home
my wife
my children
my grandchildren.

In remission
I am ashamed
I am not
light-hearted.

I long for the expansive
feeling I had
when I thought
I was leaving the world.

i.

癌の治療中に

自分が
この世を去ることを実感して
この世を去るときには
何もかも
すべて
家も
妻も
子供たちも
孫たちも
すべて
失うことになるのを
知った。
そして
もっと
軽やかに
生きればよかったと
後悔した。
この世を去る
と思ったときに
感じた
あの広々とした心が
懐かしい。

ii.

A friend of mine came over

to congratulate me
on my recovery
from cancer.
She is a retired GP
We went for a walk.
She said,
"You walk funny.
Like you have Parkinson's."

ii.

癌の治療が

終わって
恢復祝いに
元開業医だった
友人が
訪ねてきてくれた。
いっしょに
散歩に出たら
僕の歩き方がおかしい
パーキンソン病のように
歩いている
と言われた。

iii.

My legs are in prison

They want to walk freely
but something pulls
them down.

I have to spend twice
as much energy
for half
the step.

iii.

ぼくの足が

囚われてしまった
足は自由に歩きたいのに
何かが
足を抑えつけている
いつもの倍の力をいれても
半歩も
進まない。

iv.

Between actions

there are moments
when I lose myself
wondering,
What am I doing?

In the far corner
I see my socks
and think of the trouble
of putting them on.
It will take four times
longer than before.

Everything
takes more time

typing words
getting up
from the chair
cutting vegetables.

And my time is running
out. This is the riddle:
I must be fast
while going slow.

Iv.

ときどき

動作の
合間に
自分は、
いったい
ここで
何してんだろう
と茫然とする。
部屋の隅の
靴下を見ても
それを穿く手間を考えてしまう。
何をするにも
前よりずっと時間がかかる。
タイプするのも
立ち上がるのも
料理するのも
すべて
遅くなった。
そして時は
どんどん過ぎてゆく
動きは鈍くても
どう早くやるかが
工夫のしどころだ。

v.

Strange to think

I won't be
as healthy
ever again
as I was before.
I will be getting
weaker
and some day
I will perish. The whole
world will go on.

When my cancer treatment was complete
I thought I was out of the tunnel,
returning to normal, but
I went into another tunnel.

Like driving through mountains.

V.

考えてみると

不思議だ。
もう二度と
前のように
元気になることはなく
どんどん
衰弱して
その中
滅びてゆく。
それでも
世界は
何もなかったかのように
続いてゆく。

癌の治療が終わったら
トンネルを抜けたように
また前のようになる
と思っていたが
また別のトンネルに
入ってしまった。

山脈の中を通っているようだ

OLD

老い

I was living

as if I'd live forever.
At the age of seventy-four
I realized this was an illusion.

My wife said,
"I'll make it beautiful."
I asked her, "What
will you make beautiful?"
She replied,
"The garden in the next world."

Once again

I am living
and this time round
I am more aware
of life
in the shadows.

I used to think they were foolish

Now I am one of them,
and I realize they were simply
sick and old. I am
weaker but my heart
is warmer. As I die
I grow
into a better person.

I've heard

that when we die
one of the questions
we have to answer is
"Have you enjoyed your life?"

I was relieved

when I realized
it is enough
to love.
I don't need to do
anything special
to prove myself
to myself.

Jim quit his job

borrowed money
from the bank
and went
on vacation.

We sat
at the dinner table
and looked
out on cold
spring rain.
"This is not
a dress rehearsal,"
Jim said. "This is it."

"My sunset age.
I want to enjoy
my life before
it's too late."

Jim's PSA numbers
are too high.

I was listening to

an old man
talking nonsense
on CBC radio.

He wasn't up
to the points,
just trying to
please the host.

I said to myself,
"What an old fart."
Then the host said,
"He is seventy-four."

My age, exactly.

During pickleball

I feel tired
so I sit down.
Nobody else does that.
Some are older
but they keep standing.
A woman looks at me
with disgust.

I haven't told anybody,
not even the instructor,
that I have Parkinson's.
I feel I am entitled
to sit down anywhere
even in inappropriate
circumstances like pickleball.

A few minutes later
more people are sitting down.
The annoyed instructor
tells us, "Pick up the balls!"

While we rallied

intently, in the final match,
my intimidating
opponent grew
frustrated and muttered,
"I hate your dimpled racket!"
I thought, for the first time,
"Maybe I can win."

Many times a day

she asked, "What
day is it today?"
So I answered,
"Today is Sunday"
every time.
Eventually
she understood
and said,
"Oh, it's Sunday today."
Then she added,
"Is it Sunday
tomorrow?"

At the end of summer

the children depart,
leaving their shadows
with us, shadows
of this summer,
shadows of summers
before and long ago when
they still lived here.
Quickly they desert us
like the dragonflies,
leaving us melancholy
and anxious
puzzled inwardly
by love's weight.

When the flute stopped

the sound of wind came
to my ears. It sped clouds
through the sky. I thought,
this must be the sound of time.
Time passes like this.
Stagnant sometimes,
but moving like a torrent
other times, raging and changing
everything around us.

"You were young

for a long time,"
my wife says,
"and suddenly, poof,

you're an old man."

GRANDCHILDREN

Asked by her mom

what she did today,
my granddaughter

hesitated, then
she said,
"I fed ducks
in the park,"

and added,
with obvious excitement,
"I felt the feathers with my hand."

"Are you keeping me?"

asked Naoki,
my visiting grandson.
He called me
his favorite person.
I did not want to disappoint him
so I said, "Yes,
I am keeping you."
He thought about it,
and started crying
for Mommy.

Naoki-kun

My youngest grandson, said,
"I am a friend-making machine.
When I lose one friend
I make another."

My grandson

looks like an acorn
so I sing him
the Japanese song
"Donguri," meaning acorn.
He stops crying and starts
calling me Dongi.
In this way
I have become
an acorn.

Newborn, she is sleeping

her eyes closed
tight and firm.
Sometimes she shudders
like a bewildered insect,
a mystery from the other world.

Acknowledgements

Japanese Canadian poet Roy Kiyooka first suggested that I write in English instead of Japanese. As an immigrant, I was far from fluent, but a decade later, after his death, I started writing poems in English and have never stopped. I shared them with family and friends.

Two decades later, I underwent treatment for cancer. In the middle of this, I received unexpected emails from a magazine editor and a publisher, both wanting to publish my poems.

Encouraged by these developments, I wrote my *Chemotherapy Poems,* which were published in the winter 2020 edition of the *Capilano Review.*

A friend emailed me saying that she had forwarded these poems to her friend and that she had read them every day while undergoing her own chemotherapy treatment. This email sparked my desire to share my poems with a wider audience.

I thank Mona Fertig for including my work in her 2019 anthology *Love of the Salish Sea Islands* and, this year, for publishing my first book of poems. And thanks to the MTP team. It's been a wonderful surprise. I want to acknowledge Mimi Fujino, as well, for her beautiful linocut print on the cover.

Thanks to my daughter Hanako for editing my poems along with her literary friends, Meg Todd and Nadine Bachan, and for sending them to *Geist* magazine and Mother Tongue Publishing.

Yoshi Yoshihara, Masato Arikushi, Maya Koizumi, Tomas Hajek, Sean Wood, Bill Phillips, Brian Miles, Chris Taylor, Corrine Bjorge, Wendy Boothroyd, Katsuhiro Miyauchi, Kazuko Furuya, Kayo Shimazu, Hans Jungmann and many other friends, thank you all for giving me encouragement and support through the long years.

Lastly, great thanks go to my wife Jane, for always being my first reader.

Author Photo by Brian Grogan

About the Author

Matsuki Masutani is a poet and translator living on Denman Island. He moved from Tokyo to Vancouver in 1976. Ten years later he moved to Denman Island, where he eventually began writing poems in English and Japanese. He has translated Canadian works such as Roy Kiyooka's *Mothertalk* and Hiromi Goto's *A Chorus of Mushrooms*, and from Japanese into English, Kishizo Kimura's memoir, *Witness to Loss*, published by McGill-Queen's University Press in 2017. Masutani also edited the modern Japanese translation of *The Shobogenzo*, a medieval Buddhist text, for Kodansha Publishing. His poems have appeared in *Geist* magazine, *Capilano Review* and the anthology *Love of the Salish Sea Islands*.